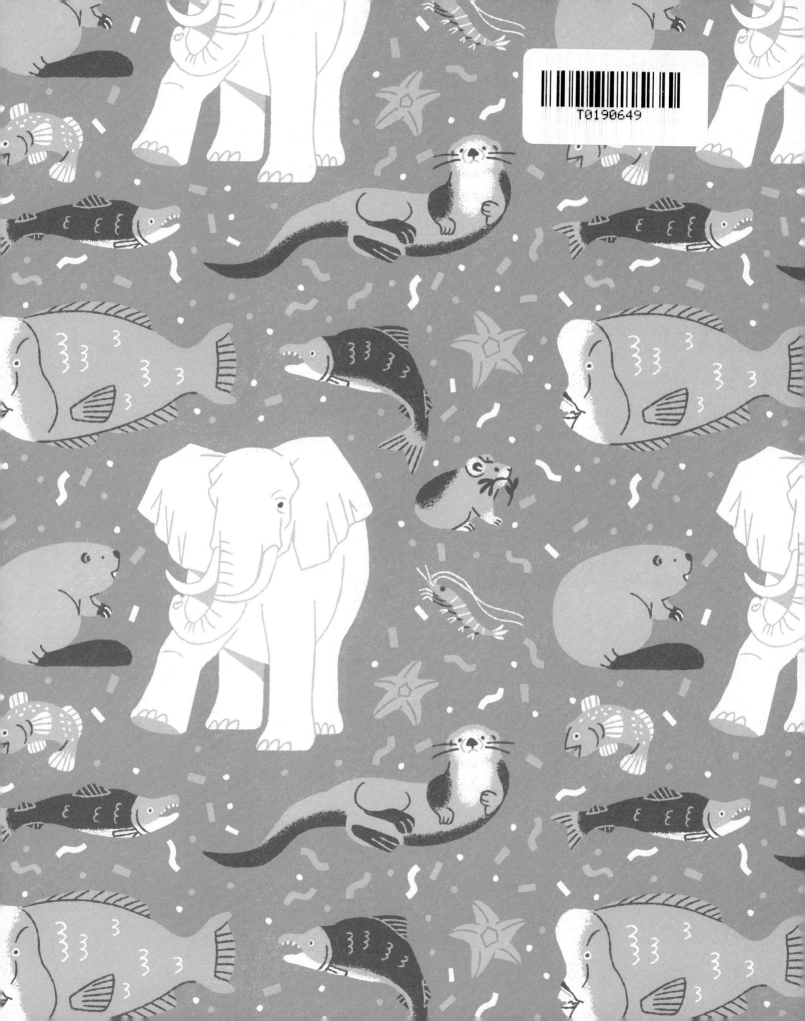

To my parents, Chris and Edwina.
Thank you for a lifetime of love and support.

—S. Wismer

To Kempchi.

—T. Po

First edition published in 2024 by Flying Eye Books Ltd.
27 Westgate Street, London, E8 3RL.

Text © Dr Sharon Wismer
Illustrations © Terri Po

Every attempt has been made to ensure any statements written as fact have been checked to the best of our abilities. However, we are still human, thankfully, and occasionally little mistakes may crop up. Should you spot any errors, please email info@nobrow.net.

Edited by Sara Forster
Designed by Sarah Crookes

1 3 5 7 9 10 8 6 4 2

Published in the US by Flying Eye Books.
Printed in Poland on FSC® certified paper.

FSC
www.fsc.org

MIX
Paper | Supporting
responsible forestry
FSC® C163799

ISBN: 978-1-83874-875-3
www.flyingeyebooks.com

WILDLIFE
IN THE BALANCE

The Species That Shape Earth's Ecosystems

Dr Sharon Wismer & Terri Po

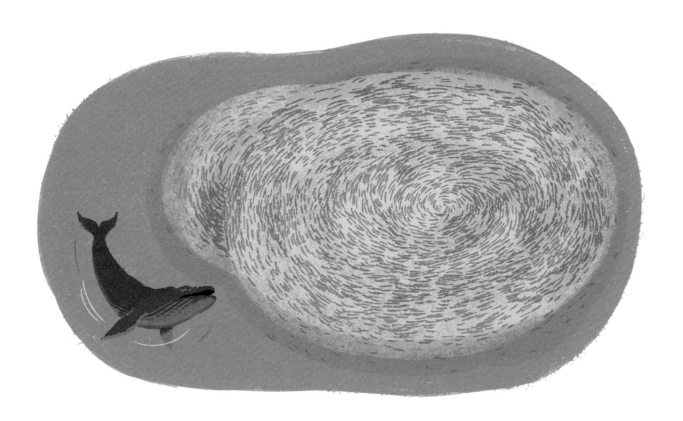

Flying Eye Books

CONTENTS

WHAT IS AN ECOSYSTEM?

An ecosystem is a community of living things, like plants and animals, the environment they live in, like soil or water, and the many interactions between them. Ecosystems are found on land, in freshwater, and in the ocean. They can be small, like a neighborhood pond, or cover large areas, like the Amazon rain forest. Our whole planet is like a big puzzle made up of many different ecosystems. Each ecosystem is unique and has its own set of plants and animals that have learned how to live there.

Desert

Dry land with little plant life and well-adapted animals. These are some of the hottest places on Earth, which receive very little rainfall.

Tundra

Cold, windy, and treeless areas often found in the polar regions. These are some of the coldest places on Earth.

Tropical Forest

These forests are found near the equator where it is warm and humid. The plants here stay green throughout the year.

Temperate Forest

These are mostly broad-leaf or needle trees that grow in moderate climates. The trees here often drop their leaves in winter.

Temperate Grassland

These are areas covered in grasses with few or no trees. They are found in colder areas that experience little rainfall.

Open Ocean

Oceanic areas away from the coast and above the seabed.

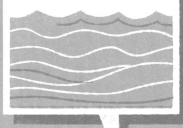

Coral Reef

These are tropical marine ecosystems. Reefs are made up of hundreds to thousands of living corals. These are some of the most diverse places on Earth.

Savanna Grassland

Found mostly in Africa, these are large areas dominated by grasses and maintained by grazing animals.

FOOD CHAINS AND WEBS

Each living thing in an ecosystem has a role to play. When animals eat, the energy in their food passes along a food chain. Food chains always start with an organism that makes food. The arrows in food chains show the flow of energy from one organism to another.

Food chain in the African savanna

Producers, like plants and algae, use sunlight to make their own food through a process called photosynthesis, which powers the rest of the ecosystem.

Consumers, like animals or humans, eat plants or other animals. There can be more than one type of consumer in a food chain.

Decomposers, like fungi, insects, and bacteria, are organisms that break down animal waste, dead plants, and animals. They return nutrients to the soil, where new plants grow.

WHO EATS WHOM?

An ecosystem contains many different food chains. Most animals eat more than one kind of food, so food chains become interconnected to form a food web. The arrows in food chains show the flow of energy from one organism to another.

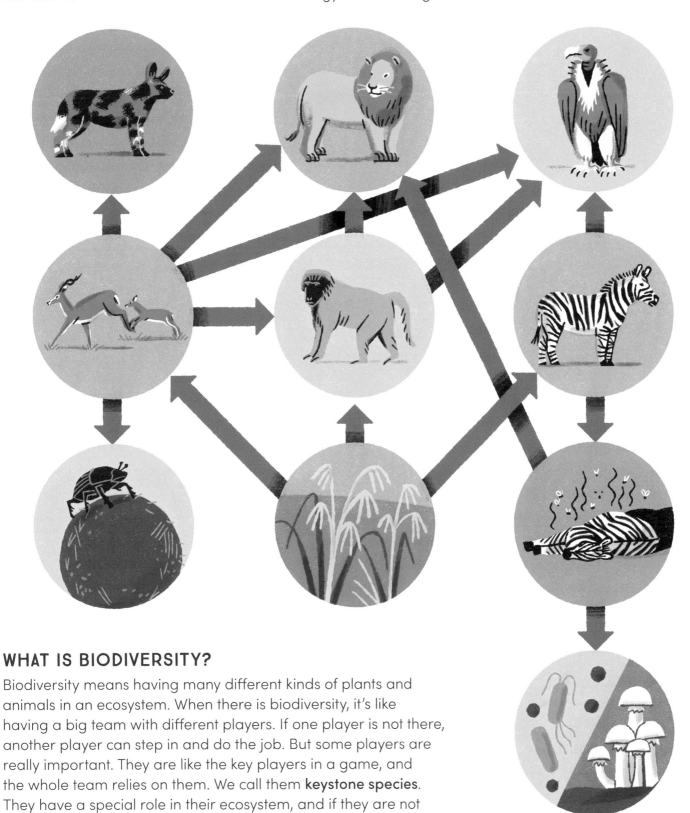

WHAT IS BIODIVERSITY?

Biodiversity means having many different kinds of plants and animals in an ecosystem. When there is biodiversity, it's like having a big team with different players. If one player is not there, another player can step in and do the job. But some players are really important. They are like the key players in a game, and the whole team relies on them. We call them **keystone species**. They have a special role in their ecosystem, and if they are not there, it can affect the whole community of plants and animals.

DISCOVERY OF KEYSTONE SPECIES

In the 1960s, biologists began asking some simple questions about the natural world. They knew that land was covered in plants but wondered why plant-eating animals didn't end up eating all the vegetation on our planet. They also began to wonder what would happen when certain animals are removed from a place. A scientist named Professor Robert Paine studied the vibrant rock pools along the Washington State coastline and found something interesting. He discovered that not all animals in a food web are equally important. Some animals play a bigger role in keeping the ecosystem balanced.

The rock pools were home to sixteen different species, including the top predator, the ochre sea star, mussels, limpets, barnacles, anemones, sponges, and sea slugs.

Prof. Paine removed ochre sea stars from half of the rock pools each month for several years. Every year, the total number of species in the rock pools without sea stars became smaller.

After five years, these rock pools only contained a single species—mussels! Their population exploded, as they were no longer being eaten by sea stars. The mussels were so dominant they pushed all other life from the rock pools, even algae.

Prof. Paine's experiments showed how a single predator can drastically impact all other members in an ecosystem. He coined the term **keystone species**, taking the name from the most important rock in a stone arch. Remove the middle rock and the whole arch comes tumbling down. That's how important the keystone species is in keeping an ecosystem balanced.

FRIENDLY YET FIERCE

A little farther up the coast, in the waters of the northern Pacific Ocean, young scientist James Estes (with help from Prof. Paine) discovered another keystone species—the sea otter! Sea otters may look fluffy and cute, but they are really strong and fierce hunters. They eat spiky sea urchins that live on the ocean floor and eat seaweed called kelp. As Estes discovered, sea otters are actually very important for keeping kelp forests healthy.

Kelp forests support many species, including fish, crabs, sea stars, harbor seals, Stellar sea lions, and bald eagles, and are even visited by orca and gray whales.

THE FORESTS OF THE OCEAN

In the Aleutian Islands of Alaska, sea otters are only found on some of the islands.

It is here that James Estes discovered that islands with lots of sea otters were also home to healthy, flourishing kelp forests.

In contrast, islands with no sea otters were ravaged by urchins. There was no kelp and no life, just a barren sea floor covered with spiny creatures.

Without predatory sea otters, urchin numbers grew and they grazed unchecked, until the kelp forest was destroyed. When the kelp disappeared, many other animals that lived there also disappeared. It was like a big chain reaction. Scientists call this a "**trophic cascade.**"

APEX PREDATORS

Apex predators are like the kings and queens of the animal world. They are at the very top of the food chain, which means they don't have any animals that hunt or eat them. These special predators are important for keeping the balance in an ecosystem. They control the populations of other animals by hunting and eating them.

When an apex predator is removed from an area it can upset the balance of the whole ecosystem. This is what happened in Yellowstone National Park. The park's apex predators, gray wolves, were hunted until they were eliminated from the park by the 1920s.

With wolves gone from Yellowstone, elk had no predators, and their numbers grew and grew. These large deer eat grasses, as well as shrubs, bark, and the shoots of young trees. Without their natural predators, elk became fearless and grazed until the landscape was barren.

In 1995, scientists relocated wild wolves from Canada and Montana to the park and released them. By reintroducing wolves to Yellowstone, the knock-on effect (a trophic cascade) happened, restoring balance to the ecosystem.

Wolves hunted, killed, and ate elk. Wolves usually target weak or old elk, so the Yellowstone elk population became stronger and more resilient.

Grizzly bears, ravens, and eagles scavenged on wolf kills.

With fewer elk, aspen and willow trees were able to grow again.

With big, healthy trees, beavers were able to create dams again.

Beaver dams created new habitats for ducks, amphibians, fish, reptiles, and river otters.

Trees provided places for songbirds to nest, and brought back migratory birds.

MEET THE KEYSTONES

Ecologists soon realized that keystone species don't have to be predators. In fact, some species of plants, birds, insects, and grazing animals are types of keystone species.

HERBIVORES

By grazing and eating plants, herbivores can shape habitats, acting as a keystone species.

Wildebeest herds keep African grasslands short and fertilized, which leads to fewer wildfires and therefore more trees.

PLANTS

Even plants can be a keystone species. They often provide food or a habitat for other species to thrive.

Fig trees in the tropical rain forests of Southeast Asia are critical for many fruit-eating animals, including bats, monkeys, and birds.

Unlike other trees, fig trees provide food year-round, while their roots stabilize the soil and prevent landslides.

PREY

Some animals are called prey because they are food for other animals. They play a very important role in the food web. Many different species rely on these prey animals for their survival. Without them, the whole ecosystem would be affected.

In the forests of North America, animals such as lynx, coyote, fox, hawks, and owls rely on snowshoe hares for survival.

WORKING TOGETHER

Species that work together to keep an ecosystem running are called keystone mutualists.

When a bee visits flowers to feed, it spreads pollen between each flower, pollinating the plant.

Without bees, the plants wouldn't be able to reproduce and create seeds. So bees and plants depend on each other for survival.

HABITAT MODIFIERS

Animals or plants that change how a place looks or is shaped are called ecosystem engineers.

The underground tunnels that prairie dogs dig help many different species in their ecosystem.

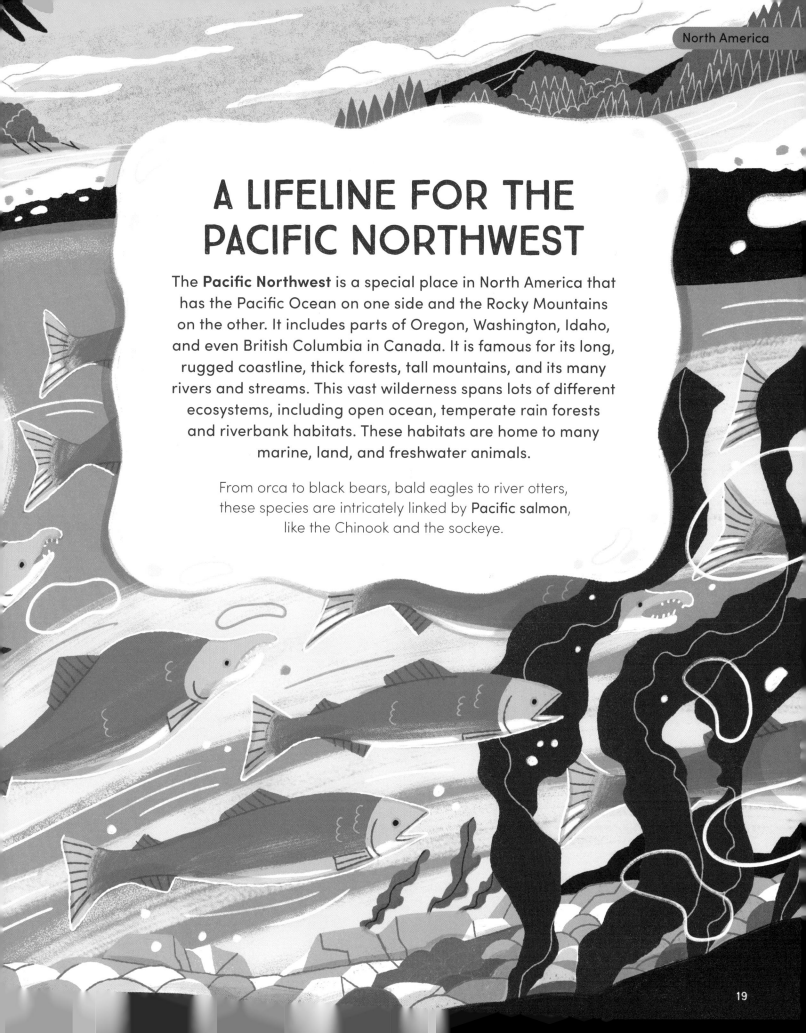

A LIFELINE FOR THE PACIFIC NORTHWEST

The **Pacific Northwest** is a special place in North America that has the Pacific Ocean on one side and the Rocky Mountains on the other. It includes parts of Oregon, Washington, Idaho, and even British Columbia in Canada. It is famous for its long, rugged coastline, thick forests, tall mountains, and its many rivers and streams. This vast wilderness spans lots of different ecosystems, including open ocean, temperate rain forests and riverbank habitats. These habitats are home to many marine, land, and freshwater animals.

From orca to black bears, bald eagles to river otters, these species are intricately linked by **Pacific salmon**, like the Chinook and the sockeye.

FROM STREAM TO SEA

Pacific salmon have a very unusual life cycle. They start their lives in freshwater streams before swimming out to the ocean. There, they feed, grow, and live for most of their lives before finally returning to the stream they were born in to spawn (lay their eggs) and die.

Salmon dig shallow nests in gravel riverbeds to lay their eggs.

Tiny, young salmon are called fry. Fry are a key predator of insects. They keep insect numbers under control. Fry are also an important food source for larger fish, mink, river otters, and many birds, like great blue herons and double-crested cormorants.

Once they gain their silver scales and adapt for life in salt water, they are called smolts. They are now ready to head to the ocean.

OPEN OCEAN

As salmon become larger, so do their predators. In the open ocean, salmon are an important food source for sharks, seals, sea lions, and the endangered southern resident orca. Unlike other orcas, this endangered group feeds almost entirely on Chinook salmon. Sadly, there are only seventy-five individuals left in the wild.

Humans are also a major consumer of Pacific salmon.

THE SALMON RUN

When salmon become adults and are ready to have babies, they swim from the ocean back to fresh water. It's a tough journey for them. Some types of salmon change their appearance during this time. They turn from silver to a bright red color, and the male salmon grow a hooked jaw called a kype. A kype helps male salmon compete with other males to find a female partner.

When bears drag their catch into the forest to feed, salmon carcasses fertilize the surrounding vegetation, which creates a stronger and healthier forest for all.

Animals like wolves, bald eagles, and bears all feed on migrating adult salmon.

After spawning, the male and female adult salmon die, supplying the river habitat with nutrients.

Salmon eggs are particularly loved by racoons, rainbow trout, and wild ducks.

SENTINEL OF THE SOUTHWEST

The **Sonoran Desert** is a large, subtropical desert in North America that stretches across parts of Arizona, California, and Mexico. It's a very hot and dry place, but surprisingly, it has many special plants and animals. This is because the desert gets rain two times a year, which helps the plants and animals survive and grow.

Peppered across the dry landscape, **saguaro cacti** can be seen reaching their thorny arms toward the sky. Saguaro cacti are an important part of the Sonoran Desert's unique ecosystem, providing food, water, and shelter to more than 100 different species.

KING OF THE CACTUS

The saguaro cactus is endemic to the Sonoran Desert. This means they only grow in this particular desert. Saguaro cacti are the largest cactus species in America, often growing over forty feet tall. Most saguaro live to between 150 and 175 years. Scientists believe that some may live for more than 200 years.

SLOW AND STEADY

Although they reach tall heights, saguaro grow very slowly, and gradually change over time.

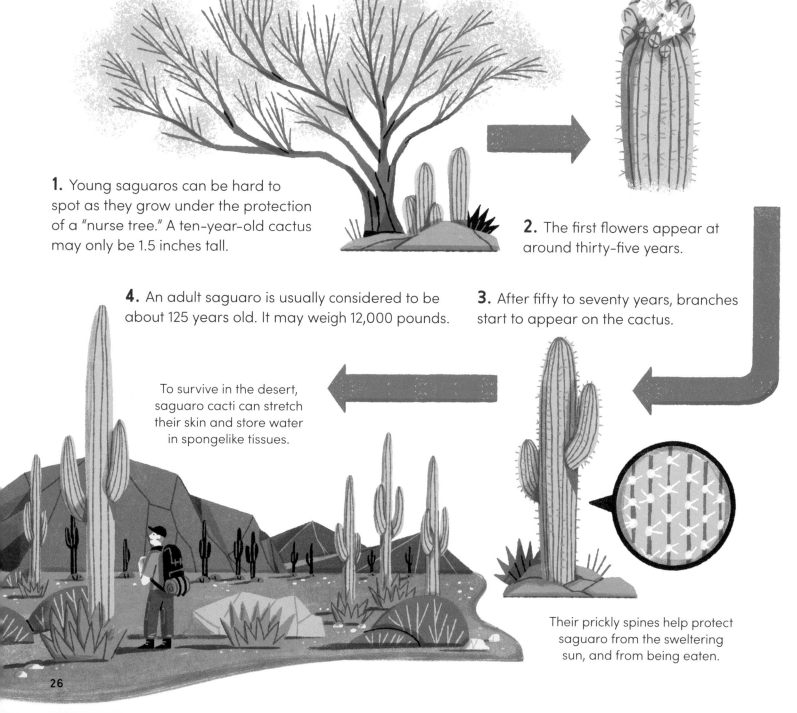

1. Young saguaros can be hard to spot as they grow under the protection of a "nurse tree." A ten-year-old cactus may only be 1.5 inches tall.

2. The first flowers appear at around thirty-five years.

4. An adult saguaro is usually considered to be about 125 years old. It may weigh 12,000 pounds.

3. After fifty to seventy years, branches start to appear on the cactus.

To survive in the desert, saguaro cacti can stretch their skin and store water in spongelike tissues.

Their prickly spines help protect saguaro from the sweltering sun, and from being eaten.

SWEET NECTAR

The saguaro cactus blooms for just a single day. In late spring, white flowers emerge on their branching arms. Pollen and nectar from the flowers are important sources of food for desert pollinators.

The flowers are pollinated by birds and insects during the day.

The flowers are pollinated by bats at night. The lesser long-nosed bat, which migrates all the way from central Mexico to the Sonoran Desert, relies on the saguaro to survive.

27

FROM FLOWER TO FRUIT

The ruby-red fruits of the saguaro cactus ripen in the summer and become food for many hungry animals. These fruits appear during the hottest and driest months of the year, when it is hard for animals to find food.

The fruits on the cactus are eaten by birds, bats, and insects.

Fruits that fall to the ground are eaten by mammals such as the piglike javelina, and reptiles like desert tortoises.

Some animals, like jackrabbits, packrats, and bighorn sheep, eat the juicy flesh of young saguaro plants to get water and stay hydrated.

A HAVEN FOR BIRDS

The saguaro cactus is also a great source of shelter for many desert birds.

Woodpeckers peck nest holes in the saguaro's stems using their pointy beaks. They use these safe, cool spaces to lay their eggs and raise their chicks.

Bigger birds, like red-tailed hawks, perch on the cacti to spot prey on the ground below. They also build their nests among the plant's many branching arms. When they've finished using their nests, other birds like ravens and great horned owls will use them.

Abandoned woodpecker holes are then used by many other bird species, like American kestrels, elf owls, and purple martins.

A FISH THAT SHAPES THE REEF

Stretching for more than 1,430 miles, Australia's **Great Barrier Reef** is the largest living structure in the world. It's home to countless colorful reef fish, sharks, and rays to invertebrates like octopus, shrimp, jellyfish, and even tiny, decorative worms. This biodiverse ecosystem exists thanks to a special reef fish, the **parrotfish**.

Parrotfish spend most of their day foraging, and are often found swimming together in large schools. Using their special beaks, they spend their days providing an underwater gardening service.

CORAL GARDENERS

Parrotfish have a special set of jaws to bite through rock-hard corals. Their teeth are fused into a beak that is made up of a very strong material called fluorapatite. They use their beaks to scrape away at algae and bite off bits of coral. This might sound quite destructive, but the parrotfish are playing a vital role in maintaining a healthy coral reef ecosystem.

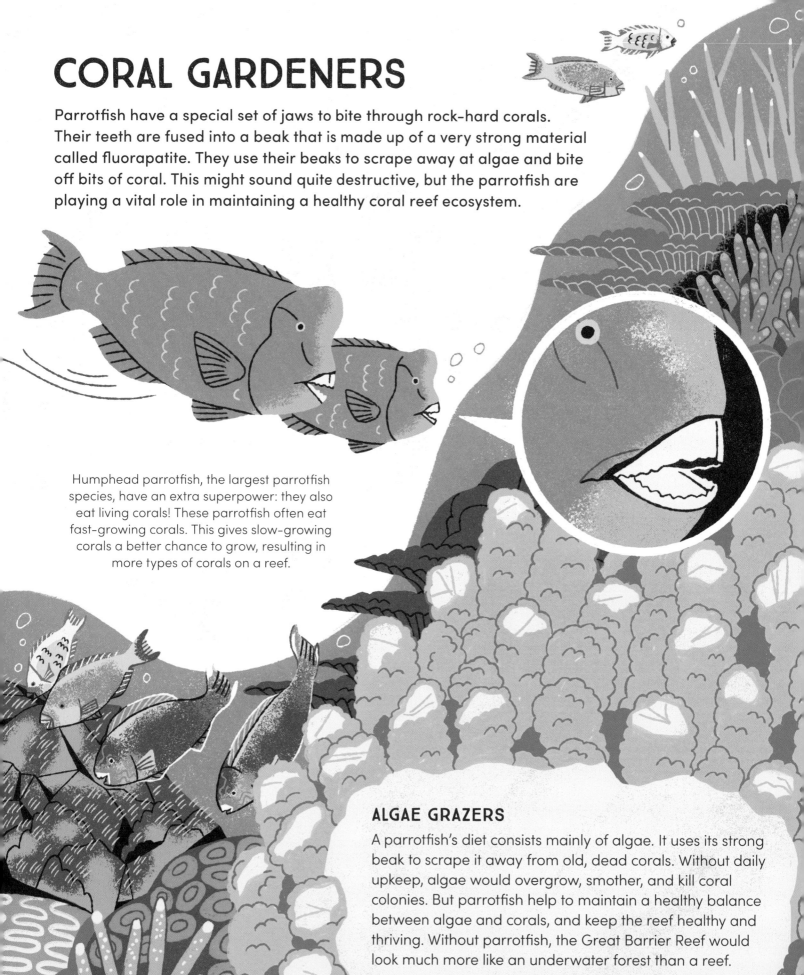

Humphead parrotfish, the largest parrotfish species, have an extra superpower: they also eat living corals! These parrotfish often eat fast-growing corals. This gives slow-growing corals a better chance to grow, resulting in more types of corals on a reef.

ALGAE GRAZERS

A parrotfish's diet consists mainly of algae. It uses its strong beak to scrape it away from old, dead corals. Without daily upkeep, algae would overgrow, smother, and kill coral colonies. But parrotfish help to maintain a healthy balance between algae and corals, and keep the reef healthy and thriving. Without parrotfish, the Great Barrier Reef would look much more like an underwater forest than a reef.

HELPING BABY CORAL

Parrotfish don't just help keep algae under control on the reef! Their foraging also helps the reef expand.

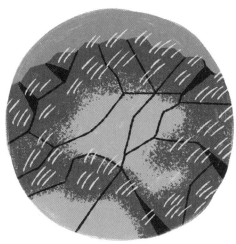

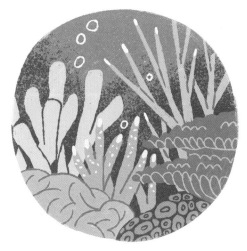

Each time a parrotfish takes a bite or "scrape" from the reef, they create a small clearing.

Incoming coral larvae need areas that are free of sand and algae to settle and grow.

Parrotfish create the perfect place for new coral growth, allowing the reef to continue to expand.

BITE, EXCRETE, REPEAT

Parrotfish have a second set of jaws in their throats that acts like a mill that grinds coral into a fine powder. Coral goes in and sand comes out. Parrotfish deposit corals back to the reef in the form of white, powdery sand. This fish poop is what creates tropical beaches that, over time, form small islands home to many plants and animals.

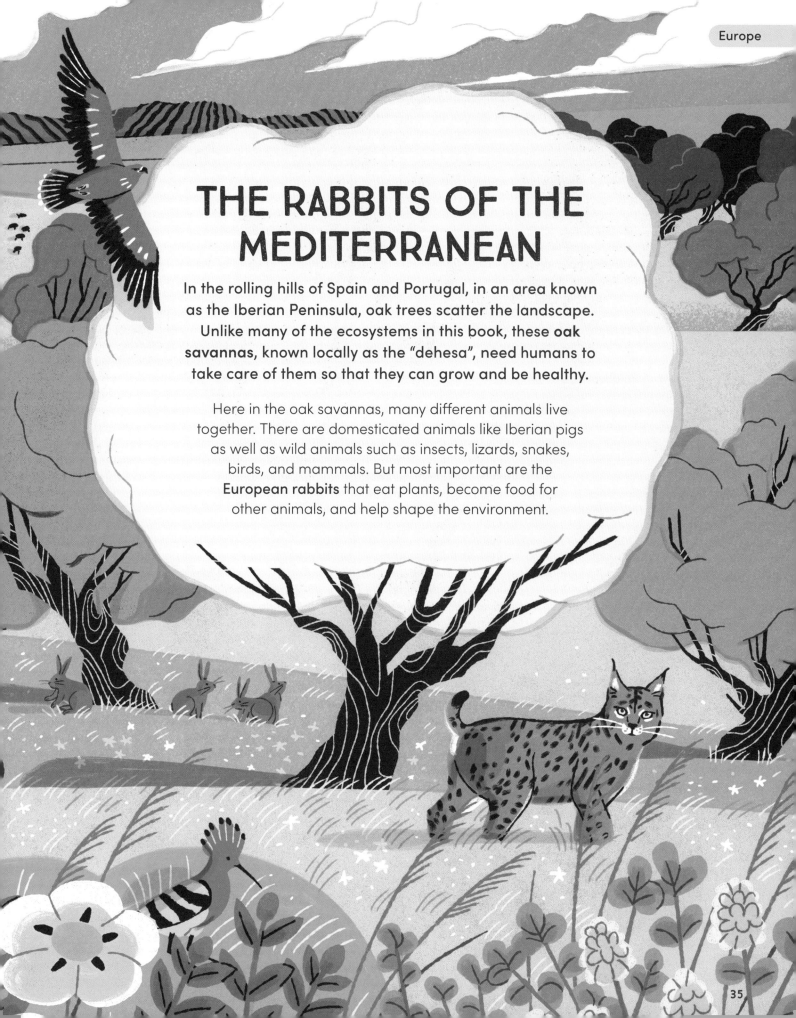

THE RABBITS OF THE MEDITERRANEAN

In the rolling hills of Spain and Portugal, in an area known as the Iberian Peninsula, oak trees scatter the landscape. Unlike many of the ecosystems in this book, these **oak savannas**, known locally as the "dehesa", need humans to take care of them so that they can grow and be healthy.

Here in the oak savannas, many different animals live together. There are domesticated animals like Iberian pigs as well as wild animals such as insects, lizards, snakes, birds, and mammals. But most important are the **European rabbits** that eat plants, become food for other animals, and help shape the environment.

SHAPING PLANT COMMUNITIES

When rabbits eat, they scratch and dig in the ground to find the food they like. This creates empty spaces where new plants can grow. When rabbits poop, their droppings help fertilize the land by bringing nutrients to the soil. Their droppings have tiny seeds that can grow into more than seventy different types of plants.

A MEAL FOR MANY

European rabbits are prey for more than forty species of predators. They are eaten by foxes, wild boar, Egyptian mongoose, stoats, snakes, and Iberian lynx, and raptors, like owls, vultures, and eagles.

Rabbit droppings feed invertebrates, like dung beetles.

But how do European rabbits survive when almost everything wants to eat them? With strong legs and clawed feet, rabbits can run fast and change direction swiftly, while high-set eyes and a flexible neck allows them to spot predators more easily. Rabbits also reproduce very often and have lots of offspring.

IN NEED OF A HELPING HAND

Sadly, the number of European rabbits in the Iberian Peninsula is getting smaller and smaller. They are facing problems like getting sick, being hunted too much, and losing their homes. They are listed as endangered, and are at risk of extinction. But we can help! One way is by making special piles of branches and mounds of soil for rabbits to hide and live in safely. When we take care of the rabbits, we also help other animals like the endangered Iberian lynx and Spanish imperial eagle, who depend on rabbits for their food.

A SAFE HIDEAWAY

Rabbits have special homes underground called warrens. These are a network of tunnels and burrows that go on for a long way and have many entrances. Many other animals, such as toads, lizards, mice, and badgers, also use these hiding places as nests or shelters. It's like a big underground neighborhood where lots of different animals live together!

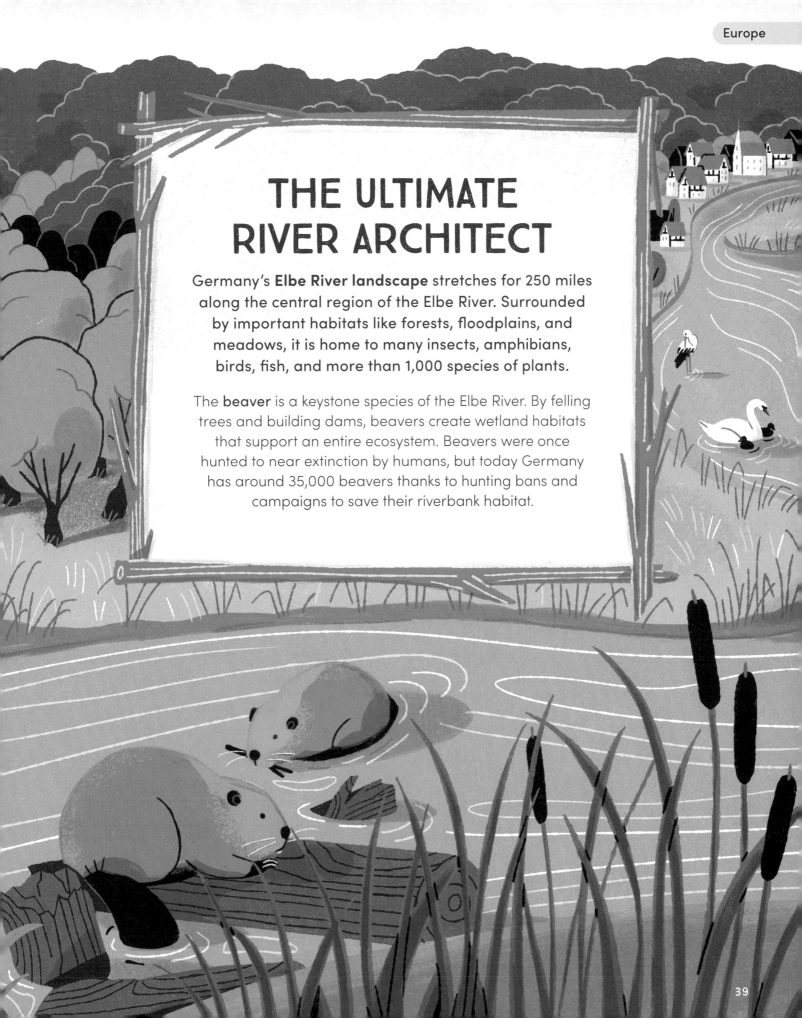

THE ULTIMATE RIVER ARCHITECT

Germany's **Elbe River landscape** stretches for 250 miles along the central region of the Elbe River. Surrounded by important habitats like forests, floodplains, and meadows, it is home to many insects, amphibians, birds, fish, and more than 1,000 species of plants.

The **beaver** is a keystone species of the Elbe River. By felling trees and building dams, beavers create wetland habitats that support an entire ecosystem. Beavers were once hunted to near extinction by humans, but today Germany has around 35,000 beavers thanks to hunting bans and campaigns to save their riverbank habitat.

BUILT FOR WATER

Beavers are rodents built for living in the water! They have strong hind legs with big, webbed feet, a sturdy tail that moves like a boat's rudder, a set of transparent eyelids that work like goggles, and a thick, waterproof fur coat. They can hold their breath underwater for fifteen minutes!

THE BUSY, BUSY BEAVER

Beavers are skilled, hardworking builders. They build dams across streams using trees, branches, rocks, and mud.

Dams can turn small streams into ponds and lakes, which provide excellent areas for other animals to use and thrive.

Beaver dams act as a natural filter system for the water, providing clean water to plants, animals, and humans downstream.

Beaver dams slow the flow of water, flooding the surrounding landscape and creating a beaver pond!

Inside their beaver pond, beavers build a special home called a lodge. It's where they live, keep their food, and raise their babies. Beaver ponds raise the water level of the stream, ensuring the entrances to their lodge remains underwater. This protects beavers against land predators like foxes and wolves.

ECOSYSTEM ENGINEER

As an ecosystem engineer, beavers transform the landscape they live in. Their dams slow down waterways and begin to create wetlands. These wetlands become homes for many different plants and animals, and the whole river area becomes a lively and thriving place.

IN THE POND

Beaver ponds contain lots of rotting leaves called leaf litter, and plant life. This creates a great home for baby fish to hide among the leaves, and for frogs to lay their eggs. The calm waters in the pond also provide perfect places for waterfowl, like ducks, to build their nests.

These beaver ponds are full of insects and fish, making them the perfect spot for river otters, mink, and waterfowl to find food.

AROUND THE POND

When beavers remove trees around the pond, it creates sunny spots that are perfect for amphibians. These animals need the sun to warm their bodies because they can't control their own body temperature.

ABOVE THE POND

The trees surrounding the ponds are filled with insects, provide food for woodpeckers, and are a useful lookout perch for birds of prey.

THE BIG ROLE OF CHINA'S LITTLE PIKA

The **Qinghai-Tibetan Plateau** is the highest and largest plateau in the world, stretching across all of Tibet and large sections of southwestern China. It has vast grasslands and majestic mountains. It is often called Asia's "water tower," as many big rivers, like the Yellow, Yangtze, and Mekong, start there. At first glance, the plateau may look empty, but it is actually home to many special animals like the elusive snow leopard and wild yaks.

The **plateau pika** is a small, burrowing mammal. They play such an important role in their ecosystem that the benefit can be seen far away downstream.

A PEST NO MORE

Plateau pikas are fluffy little animals that look a lot like rabbits. They are social animals that live in family groups. Pikas make their homes in burrows. Sadly, some farmers see pikas as pests and harm them with poison. But scientists have found out that pikas are really important for the grassland and should be protected. They help keep the ecosystem healthy!

CRITICAL FOOD SOURCE

Pikas have many predators that like to eat them, such as Pallas's cats and mountain weasels. When there are lots of pikas around, there are also lots of predators. But when people harm pikas and they disappear, their predators also go away. The predators need pikas as their main food to survive.

A COSY HOME FOR BIRDS

The plateau doesn't have many trees, but it has lots of grasslands. Since there aren't many trees, some birds can't build their nests. But they've found a clever solution! Birds like snowfinches and ground tits make their nests in the cosy burrows of pikas. However, when people harm pikas, their burrows collapse, and the bird species that rely on them can't find nesting sites anymore.

FLOOD PROTECTION

When pikas burrow, they loosen the soil so that it acts like a sponge that can store lots of water. This helps reduce flooding downstream during the wet season, and makes it less likely that rivers will dry up at other times of the year. By loosening the soil, pikas are protecting millions of people downstream who otherwise might be at risk of seasonal flooding and water shortages.

A FUTURE FOR THE PIKA?

Scientists are working hard to change how people feel about pikas. Hopefully one day pikas will be thought of as heroes, not pests. Once the value of the pika is recognized, conservation programs can start to boost pika numbers in the wild, allowing this broken ecosystem to heal.

WHERE THE RIVER MEETS THE SEA

The **Sundarbans** is the biggest mangrove forest in the world. It grows where three rivers, the Brahmaputra, Ganges, and Meghna, meet in the Bay of Bengal, and stretches across the border of Bangladesh and India. When the tide is high, the forest gets flooded with salty seawater, but when the tide is low, large mudflats are revealed. This forest is home to many species of mollusks, crustaceans, fish, reptiles, birds, and mammals. Some of them are even endangered, like the Royal Bengal tiger, the Ganges river dolphin, and the northern river terrapin.

The **mangrove trees** in the Sundarbans provide shelter for young marine life and serve as feeding grounds for many species. They are the heart of this ecosystem, keeping it alive and thriving.

LIFE IN THE TIDAL ZONE

Mangrove trees grow in a special place where the rivers meet the salty waters of the sea. The soil there doesn't have much air, and it's really soft. But the mangrove trees have special roots that help them survive. These roots grow both in the ground and above it. The roots above the ground collect oxygen from the air around them and share it with the roots below. It's like the trees are breathing through their roots! They also help the trees stay strong and not fall down in the soft, muddy soil.

A NURSERY FOR BABY FISH

Mangrove trees have lots of roots that create a safe home for many fish. Baby fish find plenty of food to eat and a safe place to hide among the roots. It's like a special nursery just for them! When the fish grow bigger and stronger, they leave the mangrove and swim out into the ocean.

THE COAST GUARD

Mangrove forests have strong, tangled roots that do amazing things. First, they protect the land, animals, and the people living there from big natural disasters like tsunamis and cyclones. It's like a big shield. Second, the mangroves clean up the water by taking away bad stuff called pollutants, and they also collect dirt and nutrients from rivers. This makes the water cleaner and healthier for the animals living there and nearby.

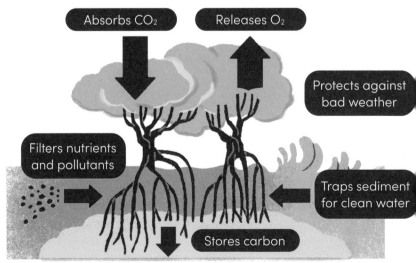

Absorbs CO_2

Releases O_2

Protects against bad weather

Filters nutrients and pollutants

Traps sediment for clean water

Stores carbon

FEEDING FRENZY

Mangrove forests are special homes for many different animals. There are hundreds of species living here! In these forests live Royal Bengal tigers. They eat deer called chital, and the deer eat the plants that grow above the water. In the water, there are tiny creatures called plankton. They are food for shrimp, and then the shrimp become food for fish. The fish are hunted by river dolphins. Fiddler crabs eat tiny bits of leftover waste called detritus and the crabs are also food for birds like ibis and kingfishers.

Like rain forests, mangroves are important ecosystems for combating climate change. They collect and store vast amounts of carbon dioxide, the greenhouse gas that is warming the Earth, from the atmosphere.

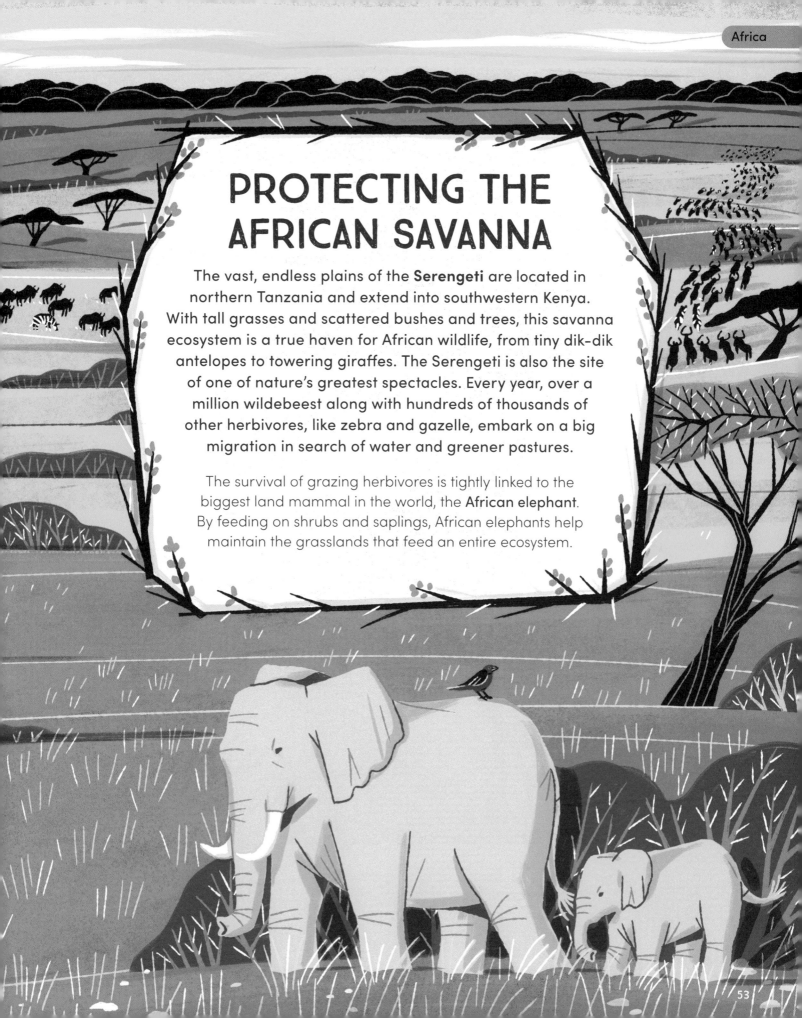

PROTECTING THE AFRICAN SAVANNA

The vast, endless plains of the **Serengeti** are located in northern Tanzania and extend into southwestern Kenya. With tall grasses and scattered bushes and trees, this savanna ecosystem is a true haven for African wildlife, from tiny dik-dik antelopes to towering giraffes. The Serengeti is also the site of one of nature's greatest spectacles. Every year, over a million wildebeest along with hundreds of thousands of other herbivores, like zebra and gazelle, embark on a big migration in search of water and greener pastures.

The survival of grazing herbivores is tightly linked to the biggest land mammal in the world, the **African elephant**. By feeding on shrubs and saplings, African elephants help maintain the grasslands that feed an entire ecosystem.

GRANDMOTHER KNOWS BEST

Elephants live in groups called herds. These herds are made up of mothers, their babies, and other family members. The most important elephant in the herd is called the matriarch. She is the oldest, biggest, and wisest elephant, and knows the best places to find food and water in the Serengeti. She leads the herd to tasty shrubs and trees, like acacia trees, which they love to eat. The matriarch also teaches young elephants how to stay away from danger.

MAINTAINING GRASSLANDS

Elephants love to eat small trees called saplings. But when they munch on them, something amazing happens! They stop the trees from growing big and turning the savanna into a thick forest. Keeping grasslands open is important for many Serengeti animals like zebras, wildebeest, and impalas to survive.

Elephants are quite destructive when they eat. They knock down trees, tear and break branches, and uproot bushes. In doing so, they create complex microhabitats on the ground where frogs, lizards, and spiders can thrive.

ELEPHANT DUNG

Elephants spend the majority of their day eating, and what goes in must also come out . . . Elephants help plants grow by spreading seeds through their poop known as dung. The seeds grow into new grasses, shrubs, and trees. This helps all the animals in the savanna. Elephant dung is also a home for termites, crickets, and dung beetles.

WATERING HOLES

In the dry season, when there is not much water, elephants use their special skills to find it. They dig wells using their feet, trunks, and tusks. With their amazing sense of smell, they can even find water underground! These wells become lifelines for other animals, especially smaller ones who cannot find water on their own.

NAMIBIAN GOBIES SAVE THE DAY

The waters off the coast of Namibia, in southwestern Africa, are one of the most fertile ocean regions in the world thanks to the **northern Benguela Upwelling**. Upwellings happen when nutrient-rich waters from the deep ocean rise to the surface. There, nutrients cause a boom in tiny plankton that feed small fish called sardines. Like a big buffet for many hungry animals, sardines used to be a tasty treat for lots of species, like Cape gannets, Cape fur seals, dolphins, seals, and sharks. But when people caught too many sardines, their numbers went down and the whole food chain crumbled.

But don't worry! There's a fish called the **bearded goby** that came to the rescue. These little gobies stepped up and helped fix the ecosystem. They started to fill the gap left by the missing sardines. With their help, the food chain started to get back on track and everyone could enjoy a delicious meal again.

A BROKEN ECOSYSTEM

So, how did the northern Benguela change from a busy, diverse ecosystem to a place where bacteria, a few species of fish, and jellyfish became the main creatures at the top of the food chain?

Upwellings happen when the wind pushes ocean surface water away, and deeper, nutrient-rich waters come up. These nutrients cause a bloom in phytoplankton and their consumers, zooplankton.

Sardines fed on the rich plankton community and in turn, were preyed upon by many different species like African penguins, Cape gannets, Albacore tuna, Cape monkfish, Cape fur seals, common dolphins, dusky dolphins, and copper sharks.

When too many sardines were caught, there weren't enough left for other animals. This made life difficult for the predators that relied on sardines for food. The whole ecosystem was affected and needed help.

Without sardines, the number of plankton in the water became very high. Soon after, lots of jellyfish appeared, but not very many animals like to eat them. Thankfully, the bearded goby was there to help balance the ecosystem and keep things going.

THE SUPER GOBY

Too much uneaten plankton can cause an explosion of bacteria, which settles on the sea floor and creates a toxic mud. Bearded gobies are one of the few fish species that can survive in this toxic, muddy environment, and over time, their numbers have grown.

Bearded gobies spend their days on the muddy surface of the ocean floor and move up toward the ocean's surface among jellyfish at night.

Not only do bearded gobies live in toxic, muddy enivronments, they even eat them! Scientists discovered that bearded gobies were eating large amounts of mud from the sea floor, which contains bacteria, microalgae, and worms.

A CRUCIAL LINK IN THE FOOD CHAIN

But what really saved this ecosystem is that gobies also eat jellyfish! With sardines gone, bearded gobies provided the missing link. They expanded the food chain once again so that it no longer ended with jellyfish.

By eating jellyfish and bacteria, gobies fill the missing gap in the food chain.

A TASTY ALTERNATIVE

Thanks to the bearded gobies, the ecosystem in the northern Benguela is getting better. Animals like seals, cormorants, and penguins have started eating gobies instead of sardines, and this has saved their populations. Even the special Heaviside's dolphins rely on gobies for their food.

THE GIVING TREE OF THE RAIN FOREST

The **Amazon** is the largest rain forest in the world. It is so big, it spans eight different countries in South America, including Brazil, Peru, and Colombia. It is home to thousands and thousands of species, from the iconic pink river dolphin and slow-moving sloth, to many colorful birds like toucans and macaws. In total, more than 40,000 plant, 400 mammal, 1,300 bird, 2,400 fish, and 370 reptile species, and countless species of insects, call this spectacular rain forest home.

Among all this life, the **moriche palm** is one of the most important trees in the thick, green rain forest. This palm tree provides food and shelter for many rain forest animals and is very important to the people who live by the rain forest.

A TREE OF LIFE

In the early 1800s, naturalist Alexander von Humboldt came across the moriche palm while exploring South America. He was so astonished at the number of animals that were supported by a single plant species that he called the moriche palm a "tree of life."

Sulphury flycatchers build their nests high within the crown of moriche palms.

Fork-tailed palm swifts build their nests in hanging, dead palm leaves called fronds.

Moriche palms also provide a safe home for small mammals, like Spix's night monkeys and kinkajous.

Brightly colored macaws raise their young inside dead, hollow moriche palms. These macaws play an important role in the rain forest because they help spread the seeds of plants when they fly around.

FLOWERS, FRUITS, AND SEEDS

Tortoises enjoy munching on the moriche palm's flowers, while animals like the lowland tapir, maned wolf, and red-bellied macaw feast on its tasty fruit. After they've had their fill, rodents such as water rats and paca snack on the leftover seeds. Other animals like capuchins, squirrel monkeys, and woodpeckers join in the feast by gobbling up insects that live on the palm's stems and fruits. It's a big party of delicious treats for everyone!

RESOURCES FOR THE LOCALS

The moriche palm provides a wealth of resources for the local human community too. The fruits of the moriche palm can be eaten, made into a juice, or used as fishing bait. The palm's seeds are used by local artists to make handmade crafts, and the leaves are used as fuel to start fires. Plant fibers from the moriche palm are used to make woven mats and bags.

The moriche palm is known locally as *aguaje*, *buriti*, or *canangucho*.

POLLINATOR OF PATAGONIA

The **Valdivian temperate forests** in Patagonia are like a magical world of small wonders! Imagine a forest filled with ferns, bamboo, and beautiful fuchsia flowers. In this special place, you can find some of the tiniest animals you've ever seen. There's the kodkod, the smallest cat in the Americas, and the pudú, the world's smallest deer. And guess what? There's even a tiny marsupial called the monito del monte!

But there's one little bird that steals the show—the **green-backed firecrown hummingbird**. This speedy hummingbird is very important. It helps pollinate many plants in the Valdivian temperate forest. It sips nectar from flowers and carries pollen from one flower to another, helping them to grow and make more plants. The green-backed firecrown hummingbird is a superhero of the forest, spreading life wherever it goes.

FERTILIZING FOREST FLOWERS

When green-backed firecrown hummingbirds sip nectar from flowers, something amazing happens, called pollination. As the hummingbirds drink the sweet nectar, tiny specks of pollen stick to their feathers and bills. The hummingbirds then flutter from flower to flower, carrying the pollen with them, spreading it from one flower to the next. This fertilizes the plant and allows it to make seeds and fruits. So you see, it's a win-win situation! The green-backed firecrown hummingbird gets delicious nectar to fuel its energy, and the plants get the help they need to make new seeds and grow more plants.

ONE OF A KIND

Green-backed firecrowns are the only birds that feed on nectar in Valdivian temperate forests. They are responsible for pollinating up to twenty percent of the woody plants in the forest. Without the green-backed firecrown, these plants would not be able to reproduce and might become extinct. Firecrowns and the plants of the forest work together to keep the ecosystem thriving.

DESIGNED FOR HUMMINGBIRDS

Flowers pollinated by hummingbirds are often bright red, orange, or pink, which helps them stand out in a green forest. They are usually long, cylindrical, or trumpet-shaped, a perfect fit for a hummingbird bill. In the Valdivian forest, green-backed firecrowns are often seen feeding from fuchsia, Chilean fire bushes, and the copihue, the national flower of Chile.

A UNIQUE TRIO

Some Valdivian plants need more than just a hummingbird for pollination. They need a marsupial too! This is an example of where not two but three species work together.

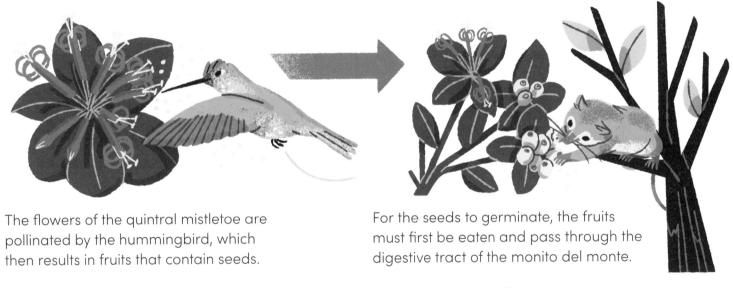

The flowers of the quintral mistletoe are pollinated by the hummingbird, which then results in fruits that contain seeds.

For the seeds to germinate, the fruits must first be eaten and pass through the digestive tract of the monito del monte.

New mistletoe plants can only grow when the seeds are dispersed through marsupial droppings on the branches of trees.

69

THE KRILL THAT POWERS THE ANTARCTIC

Antarctica is a remarkable place, known for its extreme cold, strong winds, and dry conditions. But despite these challenges, the animals that call Antarctica home have incredible adaptations that help them thrive in this beautiful yet harsh environment. Baleen whales, orca, and seals keep warm thanks to a thick layer of fat called blubber, emperor penguins have a special windproof "jacket" made of overlapping feathers, and Arctic terns are able to migrate long distances when it becomes too cold.

But perhaps the most mind-blowing adaptation is found in the tiny **Antarctic krill**. These little shrimplike creatures have a superpower—they can actually shrink their bodies! When food becomes scarce during the dark winter months, krill can reduce their size to save energy and survive until summer. Many animals, from penguins to whales, depend on krill for their survival. Without them, the entire Antarctic ecosystem would be greatly affected.

CRUCIAL CRUSTACEANS

Krill play a big role in this icy ecosystem. They are the base of the food web, which means many other animals depend on them for their meals. Whales, seals, fish, penguins, squid, and seabirds all enjoy feasting on krill. And then even bigger predators, like orcas and leopard seals, feed on those animals! Without krill, the Antarctic food web would be in trouble. If there were no krill, many animals wouldn't have enough to eat, and some could even disappear. It's like taking away the foundation of a big building—everything would collapse!

LIFE IN THE PLANKTON

Krill are special ocean creatures called zooplankton. They're also known as "drifters" in the sea because they can't swim against strong currents or waves. But they can swim up and down in the water! At night, krill use their feathery legs, called swimmerets, to swim up to the surface. There, they munch on phytoplankton and algae, which are like tiny plants that grow under the sea ice. These plants need sunlight to live. But when it's daytime and predators are out and about, krill go back down to the deeper, safer parts of the water.

TINY YET MIGHTY

Krill are small, but what they lack in size, they make up in numbers. In fact, there are so many krill in the world, they may weigh as much as all of the humans on Earth combined. Krill often travel in huge swarms made up of millions and millions of individuals. Some swarms are so big they turn the water pink and can even be spotted from space.

Krill are an excellent reminder that it is not always the biggest, strongest, or most beautiful species in an ecosystem that makes the biggest impact.

CARBON STORES

Just like plants on land, phytoplankton help take carbon dioxide out of the atmosphere and store it away. But guess what? Krill play a role in this too! When krill eat the phytoplankton, they eventually poop it out. But their poop is super special because it sinks really fast to the bottom of the ocean. And guess what? The carbon from the phytoplankton gets transferred with the poop and stored on the ocean floor. This helps keep the carbon from entering the air and making the planet hotter.

Absorbs CO_2

Stores CO_2

HOW TO HELP KEYSTONE SPECIES

While some important animals in nature are doing well, others are in danger of disappearing forever and becoming extinct. That's why people are working hard to protect them. Here are some of the ways they are helping keystone species.

REINTRODUCING SPECIES

In places where important animals have disappeared, scientists are working to bring them back. They do this through reintroduction programs. They bring animals that were born in captivity or from other areas and release them into their old homes. By doing this, they hope to help these animals return to their natural habitat and rebuild their populations.

The Eurasian beaver, the gray wolf, and the sea otter are examples of species that have been successfully reintroduced into their habitats.

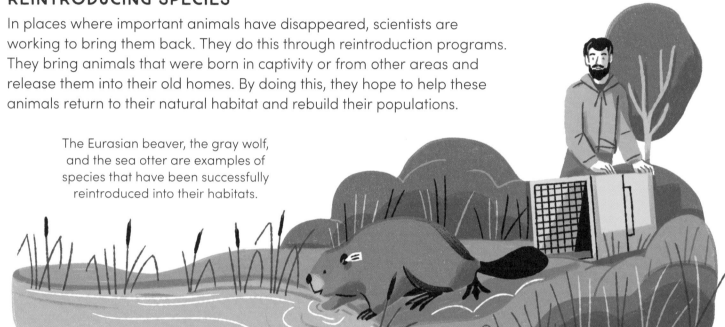

SANCTUARIES

National parks and marine-protected areas are special places where threatened species can live without being harmed. These areas are carefully protected, and harmful activities such as drilling for oil, cutting down trees, fishing, and hunting are not allowed. By stopping these activities, we give the animals a chance to grow in numbers and thrive.

Along the California and Washington State coastlines, marine sanctuaries safeguard sea otter habitats that help boost their numbers in the wild.

INNOVATIVE IDEAS

Sometimes scientists have to think outside of the box and get creative in the ways they can help wildlife. This is often the case when wildlife comes in close contact with humans.

Fish ladders are used to help Pacific salmon pass dams that have been built along their migration routes. These water-filled constructions allow fish to pass up and over dams and continue on their way.

LIMITING HUNTING AND FISHING

Sadly, many of the animals in this book have been affected by hunting, fishing, or poaching. But scientists and rangers are doing important work to protect them. Scientists are teaching people about the importance of these animals and why we should not hunt them. Meanwhile, rangers are keeping a close watch to catch poachers, remove traps, and break down their camps. They are fighting to keep the animals safe in their natural homes.

Tracking dogs are specially trained dogs that use their incredible sense of smell to track down poachers and find illegal wildlife products like tusks and horns. The dogs and their handlers work as a team, bravely patrolling the wilderness to keep these endangered species safe.

SPREAD THE WORD!

And finally, you can help too! Why not tell a friend or your classmates about some of the incredible animals you've read about in this book.

GLOSSARY

A

Adaptation Body parts or behaviors that help a living thing survive in an environment

Amphibian Any organism that can live both on land and in water

Apex predator Animals at the top of the food chain

B

Barren Empty of life

Biodiversity The variety of plant and animal life

Biologist A scientist who studies the natural world and the things in it

Bird of prey Birds that mainly use their claws (talons) to seize prey

C

Carbon dioxide A gas released into the Earth's atmosphere when fossil feuls are burned

Climate The long-term pattern of weather in a particular area

Conservation The protection of things found in nature

Crustacean An animal with a hard shell and legs, that normally lives in water, like crabs and krill

D

Domesticate To tame a wild animal or plant so it can live with people

E

Ecologist A scientist who studies ecology, the relationship between living things, and their surroundings

Ecosystem All the living and nonliving things in an area, including plants and animals, and the interactions between them

Endangered A plant or animal in danger of disappearing forever

Endemic A species that is only found in one particular area on Earth

Equator The imaginary line around the Earth that separates the north and south

Extinction The disappearance of a species from Earth

F

Fertile Capable of producing offspring or fruit

Fertilize The process of creating life

Food chain The order in which living things depend on each other for food

Freshwater Water found in ponds, lakes, rivers, streams, glaciers, icebergs, ice caps, and sheets

H

Habitat A place where things naturally live and grow

Humid The amount of water vapor in the air

I

Invertebrate Animal without a backbone or bony skeleton

K

Keystone species Organisms that play a crucial role in different habitats, and have a vital effect on the environment around them

M

Mammal An animal that breathes air, has a backbone, grows hair, and feeds milk to its young

Mangrove Trees or bushes that grow in thick clusters along seashores and riverbeds

Matriarch A female who rules a family or group

Migrate To move from one place to another

N

Naturalist A person who studies natural history

Nutrients Substances required by the body to perform its basic functions

O

Offspring The young of an animal or a person's children

Organism Any biological living system that functions as an individual life form

P

Plateau A raised area of land that is flat on top

Predator An animal that hunts and eats other animals for food and energy

R

Reproduction The production of offspring

S

Species A group of living things that can reproduce with one another

Subtropical Bordering on the tropics

T

Temperate A moderate climate

Trophic cascade Changes in the balance of an ecosystem after a trophic level (species) is removed or reduced

INDEX

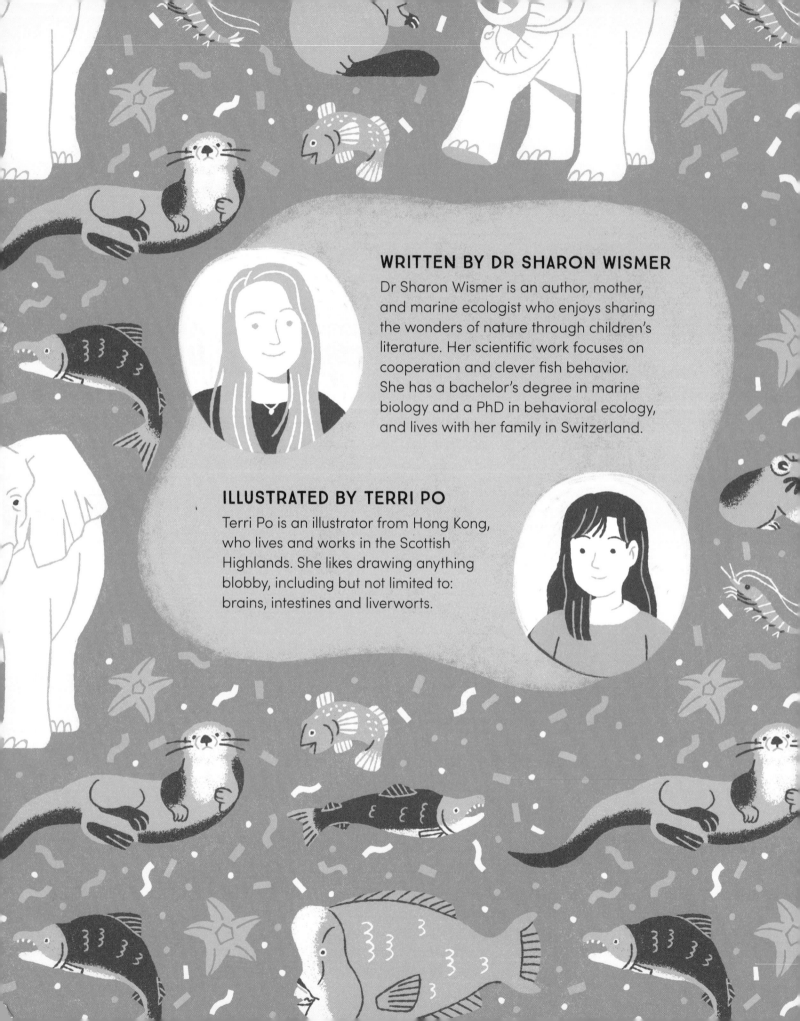

WRITTEN BY DR SHARON WISMER

Dr Sharon Wismer is an author, mother, and marine ecologist who enjoys sharing the wonders of nature through children's literature. Her scientific work focuses on cooperation and clever fish behavior. She has a bachelor's degree in marine biology and a PhD in behavioral ecology, and lives with her family in Switzerland.

ILLUSTRATED BY TERRI PO

Terri Po is an illustrator from Hong Kong, who lives and works in the Scottish Highlands. She likes drawing anything blobby, including but not limited to: brains, intestines and liverworts.